A New
PENANCE BOOK

*All booklets are published thanks to the
generous support of the members of the
Catholic Truth Society*

CATHOLIC TRUTH SOCIETY
PUBLISHERS TO THE HOLY SEE

CONTENTS

Acknowledgements

We Acknowledge with thanks, material written for the CTS by Fr J Webb, and Robert Tylerson and reproduced here. Scriptural passages from the Jerusalem Bible (DLT), and translations of text and prayers in Rites authorised by ICEL.

WHY GO TO CONFESSION?

Being reconciled

Many people find the sacrament of reconciliation (or penance, or confession - keep to the old names if you like), difficult. It is for some a rather neglected Sacrament, approached out of duty rather than with joy. There is a feeling that one is not getting the best of it, if indeed there is anything to be got out of it, over and above confession and absolution.

Our understanding of the benefits to be gained from the Sacrament of reconciliation will be heightened if we pause to consider how necessary reconciliation is. On the ordinary human level we know only too well the need to be reconciled with each other when, through our own fault, we have fallen out. We know that being reconciled is not just a matter of saying, 'Sorry', putting the quarrel behind us; we want and need to be accepted back, to be given another chance, to be thought no less of; we want to make up and to know our sorrow is accepted.

The mystery of God's love

If we need to convince ourselves of the need for reconciliation, let us not think of our sins and failings, let us rather stand by the cross with Mary our mother and the disciple whom Jesus loved and let it sink into our heart that all his pain and agony was joyfully undergone to save each of us - you and me - from our sins.

Meeting Christ himself

What he gained for us on the cross he distributes - if that is the right word - through the Sacraments. A sacrament is not just a rite or a ceremony, it is a meeting with Our Lord himself. We receive not a thing nor a quality but a person, Christ himself. In the Sacrament of reconciliation we receive the same Jesus whom we receive in Communion. He comes now as the physician of our souls, as the physician who longs to heal, to bind up our wounds and restore us to full spiritual health. Our need for forgiveness is far outmatched by his longing to impart it. He comes to heal the soul he has already died for and he comes to heal it in his own way: in the Sacrament he instituted for that very purpose.

Hope for the prodigal son

First of all, what happens when we are reconciled in the words of absolution? Put simply, Christ unites himself with us by grace. He floods our soul with his presence. Absolution is not just a judicial act, an acquittal or pardon from guilt - it has elements of all these, of course, but only because it is so much more. We receive Christ himself who comes to heal, restore and forgive the soul he has already ransomed. What happens can only be described in the language of human love or under the figure of homecoming, as in that perfect example of reconciliation, the father and his prodigal son. Imagine yourself as the prodigal son and see what hope reconciliation gives. Indeed, it might well be described as the sacrament of hope. For in it we have, if we are truly sorry, the certainty - not just the possibility - of forgiveness and the chance of a completely new start every time. And as if all this were not enough, we have the hope of attaining that measure of perfection Our Lord wills for us, through the positive graces he offers in this Sacrament.

Forgiveness

Forgiveness is accomplished by the gift of Jesus Christ to the soul; his very presence casts out sin and guilt. Just as the father threw his arms around the prodigal son and kissed him, Our Lord receives us eagerly and takes us back to himself, makes us one with him and at one with him - that's what the word 'reconcile' means. And it is he who does the reconciling, not ourselves. Our sorrow alone would be ineffective - what makes the reconciliation, is his acceptance of our sorrow and the free gift of himself. We would do well to remind ourselves that our sins have truly been cast out, and that we have been given a fresh start.

Healing and consolation

The healing aspect of reconciliation is an unending source of consolation. Even the briefest treatment of it is enough to make one realise that here we have a Sacrament tailor-made as it were for the soul's deepest needs. In short, his life-giving presence within us restores our lost integrity. In other words, we are restored to wholeness, to health, to spiritual vigour. We regain the real self that sin (which proceeds from and goes on to create a false self) had marred and blotched.

Good that comes from confession

The manifold graces here made available to us by the Light and Lover of our souls would provide food for daily meditation for weeks. You can fill out the list for yourselves, but here are the more obvious ones: our weakness is strengthened, our proneness to sin diminished, the bonds or clinging quality of sinful tendencies are loosened, the grace we have lost is restored - and more than restored; we receive encouragement, the great encouragement of knowing that his strength can and will transform our weakness; we receive the assurance that he accepts and deals with us as we are. It would not be too fanciful surely to suggest that Our Lord coaxes us towards virtue as a mother coaxes her child to do what it cannot see is for its own good - enlightening our minds to see his will more clearly and giving us the motivation to love him more dearly, giving us a deeper insight into our sinfulness, but at the same time - in case that insight sets us back - giving us a deeper awareness that his grace is abounding and to be had for the asking.

Practical suggestions

Naturally, the more you realise what there is to be gained from the Sacrament of reconciliation, the more you will want to take care that you make the most of it.

Obviously, as in every other Sacrament, Christ unfailingly gives of himself and it is always the same self. However, your own disposition determines to a considerable extent just how effectively he is received. Hence the need for a proper preparation, a simple method of confessing, and adequate follow-up. As this is just what many people find difficult, here are a few practical suggestions.

Looking forward to confession

An important part of preparation is looking forward to going to confession. Yes, looking forward. The more we look forward to an event the more we are likely to benefit from it - that's the point of Lent and Advent - and is not being restored to wholeness and soundness of soul worth looking forward to? What God works in us is cause for deep spiritual joy, and therefore well worth looking forward to.

Ask for true sorrow

The essential ingredient of the Sacrament is, from our point of view, sorrow. But we tend to forget, perhaps, that sorrow is not something we can manufacture by ourselves; it is a gift from God - so the best way to achieve sorrow is to ask for it, knowing it will never be refused. Note that we must be sorry, not feel sorry. Our feelings are only imperfectly under our control and are not always a safe guide. Real sorrow consists in acknowledging that through our own fault we have offended our maker and redeemer by going against his will. We acknowledge this in humbly asking pardon, in intending to turn away from sin and in a willingness to do our best to make up.

Examining your conscience

Having resolutely asked God to give us the grace to be sorry, let us set about deciding what to say to the Priest in the confessional. It is well to have a method of examining your conscience - the simpler the better, and one that suits you. If you are happy as you are, do not change for the sake of the experiment.

If you are not too satisfied, try using the ten commandments as a framework; or think of your failings under the headings of thought, word, deed and omission; or in the different parts of your life - work, home, family, friends. Whichever way you choose, spend no more than fifteen minutes in the actual examination - aim to be thorough without being scrupulous. And examine your conscience in the presence of God, asking him to reveal to you those areas of your life that are in need of his healing; ask him to help you to see yourself through his eyes.

Making your confession

Once you are with the Priest and have started your confession, take your time. It is an important time for you and rushing will only spoil it. Remember, too, that you are not accounting to the Priest for your sins, you are expressing sorrow for them to your heavenly Father. Direct your mind and heart to him. Since it is your Father in heaven you are primarily addressing, you need have no fear about expressing yourself. Do not worry if words fail you - honest sorrow is more important than accurate description. Anyhow, God knows what you have done better than you know yourself.

Some people find the actual process of confessing to another human being things they may not properly voice even to themselves difficult and embarrassing. The Priest understands this - after all he goes to confession himself - and will make allowances. It might help, or at least break the ice, if you said at the beginning that you find things awkward.

What to do after confession

After you have received absolution, there is still more to be done. It is important to spend five to ten minutes in prayer afterwards; this will ensure that, having had the experience of reconciliation, you will more fully appreciate its meaning. Kneel in silence and dwell upon the fact that God has made you one with him again, and thank him with all your heart. Then think ahead, think of the opportunities that you know will arise for doing good, the temptations that you are likely to meet, and ask for the grace to tackle them better. If you need to make it up with anyone, decide how and when to do so. Then say your penance. And so the process is complete.

A closer relationship with God

It must be obvious by now, having considered the effects of reconciliation, that we have in this Sacrament a wonderful means of spiritual development. But it will not help us very far on the road to perfection if we only go when we are in dire need, or if we confine ourselves to an annual Easter confession. Spiritual development or striving for perfection is nothing else than seeking a closer relationship with Our Lord, and there can be no relationship with anybody without regular personal contact.

Regular Confession

What Christ offers in this Sacrament is the very thing we need in order to avoid what is wrong and be better enabled to do what is good. It stands to reason that we need it as regularly as we need to pray. Note, as regularly, not as frequently. We need to pray more often than we need confession, but both should be done as a regular practice. We have more cups of tea than we have warm baths, but hopefully we have both regularly.

It is not necessary to go to confession every time we wish to receive Communion. We are only obliged to go if we are conscious of having sinned grievously - in case anyone still labours under misunderstanding this and, as a consequence, receives Communion far less often than they might.

How often should I go to confession?

Well, how often should we approach the Sacrament? Certainly more than once a year. Once every six months, every quarter, every month, fortnight or week - any of these patterns, or any other you wish, as long as it suits you and, most important, so long as you stick to it. You will soon find, if you have not been going regularly up to now, that once you have stuck to a definite pattern for a year, you will know whether that pattern is the right one for you and, if it is not, you will make adjustments. You will also find that regular confession creates an appetite for itself, that once you have come to experience its value, you will, genuinely and unaffectedly, look forward to confession. Once regular confession has taken root, it is rarely abandoned.

Knowing God's mercy

Good habits do away with and regular confession does,
in a general way, gradually free us from our sinfulness
- in much the same way that our bodies, our clothes and
our homes are much easier to keep clean if they are
washed and cleaned regularly. Once dirt has been left
to get ingrained, its a different kettle of fish. Among its
other effects is a deeper awareness of our own
sinfulness and failings, but this will not cause
depression and despondency because the other side of
the coin will be a greater sense of God's mercy and of
what his will for us is, together with the realisation that
he asks nothing of us without first giving us ample
grace to achieve it.

Of course you are not to expect to feel any different, or
to be able to plot progress - that is not how grace works.
Whatever progress you make is unlikely to be apparent to
yourself. You might very well come to feel that you are
more of a sinner than you realised - but that, in itself,
would be a sign of progress!

Patience and freedom

Be patient; there is no such thing as instant improvement,
and the results of being regularly reconciled to God will
be gradual and cumulative. There is, however, one thing
you can be sure about: the regular practice of expressing
sorrow and receiving certain forgiveness will put your

sins in their place and remove any false sense of enduring guilt you may have been plagued by, as you come to realise that the absolution you receive and can look forward to receiving regularly, is itself a foretaste of that complete freedom from sin and perfect union with God that he has in store for you in heaven.

Let us then resolve to see in this great and consoling Sacrament a spur towards that goal, and receive it with the enthusiasm and gratitude - and regularity - it deserves.

SACRAMENT OF RECONCILIATION - SUMMARY

Preparation

Prepare yourself for 5 or 10 minutes, usually in silence, examining your conscience. This can also be done with the help of a Scripture reading (see pp. 33-38).

Celebrating the Sacrament

Approach the priest who welcomes you, and bless yourself .
Introduce yourself, and how long it is since your last confession.
The priest may read a short passage of scripture.
The Priest will invite you to make your confession.
Make confession of your sins as simply and clearly as you can, asking forgiveness for them.
Listen attentively to any advice, encouragement and guidance the priest may have.
Accept the penance the priest proposes.
Say a prayer of sorrow (act of contrition).
Receive the absolution of your sins from the priest.
Final prayer and conclusion.

Afterwards

Spend 10 minutes in quiet prayer (see pp. 39-45). Say the prayer(s) given as part of your penance. Ask God to help you to make satisfaction for your sins.

PREPARING FOR CONFESSION

Recognising my sins

Awareness of sin is a vital part of the Christian life. I can only be free from sin when I first acknowledge it. One passage from Luke's gospel makes the point well.

'The tax collector stood some distance away, not daring even to raise his eyes to heaven; but he beat his breast and said, 'God, be merciful to me, a sinner'. This man, I tell you, went home again at rights with God; the other did not. For everyone who exalts himself will be humbled, but the man who humbles himself will be exalted'. *(Luke 18:13-14)*

The gospel parable about the seemingly good Pharisee, and seemingly sinful tax-collector gives me confidence that if I, with the tax-collector, can honestly pray: 'God, be merciful to me, a sinner', God will forgive me, whatever my sins, and they can be washed away by his forgiveness. If I am not aware of my sin, like the Pharisee, I am in a sad state; I am not at rights with God.

Have mercy on me, a sinner

If I need to be further convinced, or need more scripture to reflect on, then I need only ask, 'Who was the only person to whom Christ promised, 'This day you will be with me in paradise'? *(Luke 23:42)* Not a 'saint' in any recognisable way, but a thief, someone who knew he had done wrong and deserved punishment.

Recognising sin is the first step to the joy of being freed from sin. To start, I need to see my sin, to know that my sin is mine. I am to blame. It is my responsibility. This sin is then also mine to confess to Christ and so to be freed from it. I am not free to confess what I don't admit to owning. I have to recognise and admit to my sin before I can give it to Christ. Then he will lift the burden from me, taking my sins on his cross.

My difficulty is not only in having the courage to say 'sorry'. My problem, so often, is to recognise my sins in the first place.

Conscience

My conscience (consciousness) is my self-awareness before God. It includes an awareness of what I think, say, do, or decide not to do. It includes my perception of how I match up to God's will, and this awareness can be clear or cloudy, and true or false. Am I at one with him? Conscience isn't only to do with feelings either. It is not a matter of whether I'm weighed down with guilt, or buoyed up with the consolation of feeling good. It is an assessment I make, using all that is human within me, my understanding, my mind, my experience and so on, not just emotions.

Forming my conscience

But there is something even more important about conscience. It is about having a vision of each detail of my life, not from my point of view, but from God's. He must be asked to form my views. If my conscience were true, I would see all areas of my life in the same way that God does. God wants my conscience to be formed in union with his clear view. My part in conscience formation requires me to work to develop different aspects:

1. My knowledge of God's will (his self-revelation)
2. My awareness of myself; what I do, think, or refrain from doing (my self-awareness)
3. My awareness of what God would like me to be doing, saying, (discernment).

The first of these gives me the obligation to learn about the faith, the second gives the obligation to learn about myself, and the third gives the obligation to develop my loving relationship with God, to grow, to talk, to listen, to share and to learn. Not only are these things obligations, they are also invitations from God, to grow in love.

Role of conscience in preventing sin

St Maximus the Confessor, in the seventh century, listed five things which make a soul cut itself off from sin:

1. Fear of others
2. Fear of judgment

3. Hope of future reward
4. Love of God
5. The promptings of conscience.

It is a good itemised list. In our society, for whatever reasons, the awareness of the power of all these criteria seems weakened. There are fewer impulses to fear man and to fear judgment. Many people do not understand the great gift of hope, and often do not understand the deep love of God. As I live in this society, my awareness of sin, too, is more easily clouded, and can even be under attack. Perhaps more is demanded of the prompting of my conscience now than ever before. It is put under pressure, and at the same time I often feel I lack the discernment to be aware of sin and to react against it as I should.

Part of the training of conscience is like any other training; it works best when it is disciplined and regular. No boxer, knowing that he had a major fight coming up, would neglect a day's training, and the same is true in the Christian life. There will always be temptations, perhaps major ones when I least expect them. By daily examination I learn to recognise where the blows are likely to come from, and how to duck and avoid them.

An informed conscience

More and more, individual informed conscience is relied upon as the key to the prevention of sin, perhaps too much so. Perhaps I should mould my way of life so that more of the other factors of Maximus work together, to stop me sinning. The most effective way to prevent sin in my life is to be constantly aware of all the items in Maximus's list. Wherever human laws, or peer pressures are aligned to God's will, it is a blessing and a help to avoid sin. In the same way a true awareness that I am to be judged, a strong hope in God's kingdom, and an awareness of his overflowing love are all important. They can each help to diminish my sinfulness. I should constantly pray for each of these blessings, and thank God when they are present. Whichever of these are present, however, I can never afford to neglect conscience.

Examining my conscience

There are several problems and difficulties which regularly seem to get in the way when I try to examine my conscience. If these are a problem, it is good to recognise them, and to have some way to deal with them.

Need for humility

Sin can't be seen without humility. I need to ask God for it again and again. St Francis de Sales said that if we are truly humble, our sins will be infinitely offensive to us, since God is offended by them. If I want to grow, it means wanting to grow in humility. It may take me down unexpected paths. Because of my human nature, one effective way of growing in humility is by being humiliated, by failing, by not measuring up. When I pray for humility, I shouldn't be surprised if this is how it comes.

Too lax or too scrupulous?

St Ignatius of Loyola suggests that if the devil sees I have a delicate conscience, he seeks to make it excessively delicate (scrupulous) in order to upset me. If he sees that I have a lax conscience, he will attempt to make it more lax, so that if I ignore lesser sins, he will try to make me ignore more serious ones too. Ignatius suggests that I ask God to make me aware of the direction in which my conscience is drifting, and always try to move it back towards the right path. So if my conscience is lax, I try to be vigilant to make it more strict, and if it seems scrupulous, I am vigilant so that small sins don't unduly disturb the peace and joy which should, at some level, be the norm of Christian life.

Temptation or sin?

Temptation occurs when either my own will, or the devil, puts into my mind a proposal and makes it seem attractive. The proposal concerns something that is not virtuous, not responding to God's grace, and not according to God's will. I sin only when I consent to that proposal, when I put its short-term attractions before the eternal attractions of being with God. There will, each day, be thousands of temptations to sin trying to distract my attention from God by looking attractive. Sin is not directly to do with these attractions, but with my decision or choice to prefer, and act on, the attractive temptation, rather than God's will, love and grace.

Being honest with yourself

It is only by being honest about my sin that I can experience joy in God's forgiveness. Weakness and sin are often linked, but never identical. It is good to know what my weaknesses are. It is also good to know the psychological pressures in my life which make me more likely to commit a particular sin. The knowledge of these allows a better view of how serious a sin is, and my degree of blame, or culpability in committing it. But at the end of the day it is still sin, and I need the courage to acknowledge it as such. I ask forgiveness, and for God to give me strength to combat it.

Patience and courage with our sins

St Francis de Sales gives wise advice. He says that sudden conversions which completely free us from sin are uncommon. For most of us the usual cleansing from sin takes place only very slowly, step by step, with difficulty and patience. He compares the soul that rises from sin to devotion, to the dawning day, which at its approach does not drive out the darkness in an instant, but only little by little.

'Diseases of the soul as well as the body come racing along on horseback, but leave slowly on foot.' This is the normal pattern. Commitment and strength often chip away at habits of sin rather than overcome them completely all at once. He counsels patience and courage. The virtue of hope, rejoicing at small victories, is also a great strength.

In the battle with sin, one unexpected consolation can be the humility that the lack of success gives me, the knowledge that I'm dependant on God's grace, and that I need him.

How should I describe my sins?

Two rules of thumb for describing sin are:

1. I focus on the actual sin itself (not anybody who persuaded me to do it, not on any pressures there were, not on any circumstances which aren't relevant).

2. I describe the sin as simply as possible. I don't use words with many syllables (e.g. 'Uncharitability' has several! It is better to use words with no more than two. Short words often better get to the heart of where sin is.)

A simple, but detailed explanation is more likely to give me true insight into my sin, and make me more contrite. Candour and simplicity are great paths to both contrition and repentance. They help my conscience to be open and at rest.

Preparing for confession

Heartfelt sorrow for our sins and a determination not to sin again are at the centre of our reconciliation with Our Lord and his church. Before approaching the Priest we need to prepare ourselves by prayer and examining our conscience. The following prayer may be helpful:

Almighty and merciful God, you have brought me here in the name of your Son to receive your mercy and grace in my time of need. Open my eyes to see the evil I have done. Touch my heart and convert me to yourself. Where sin has separated me from you, may your love unite me to you again: where sin has brought weakness, may your power heal and strengthen; where sin has brought death, may your Spirit raise to new life. Give me a new heart to love you, so that my life may reflect the image of your Son. May the world see the glory of Christ revealed in your Church, and come to know that he is the one whom you have sent, Jesus Christ, your Son, Our Lord. Amen.

EXAMINING YOUR CONSCIENCE

Preparing for the sacrament

The following 'examination of conscience' may help you to compare your life with the example and commandments of Christ.

Our Lord wants us to experience a real change in our whole outlook through receiving the Sacrament of Penance; he wants us really to make up our minds to follow in the way he is leading; hating sin and loving God, as he said, with all our heart, and with all our soul, and with all our mind, and with all our strength.

'You shall love the Lord your God with all your heart, and with all your soul, and with all your mind, and with all your strength.'

When making important decisions about my way of life, have I put God first?

Am I so caught up with getting on in this world that I give no thought to God, my Father?

Have I compromised my faith by setting aside the Church's teaching and going my own way or by not asking for guidance when I am really doubtful what to do?

Have I really trusted God, especially in times of difficulty?

Have I prayed each day, morning and evening?

Is Sunday a day on which I give time to God and my faith particularly by taking a full and prayerful part in the Mass. Is my heart set on money, possessions and security?

'You shall love your neighbour as yourself'.
In my family life, do I really try to fulfil my responsibilities, as father or mother, husband or wife, son or daughter? Do I make my home a happy and loving place by being tolerant and forgiving, giving the others consideration and supporting them in their personal difficulties? Do I show proper respect for the other members of my family.

Do I scandalise others in what I say or do in their presence? Have I been faithful to my spouse?

Do I gamble for my own personal amusement to the harm of those who depend on me?

Do I take a fair share of responsibility for others, the less fortunate, sick and oppressed?

Do I despise others, particularly those of other races or religions? Do I use others for my own ends?

Have I paid my taxes? Do I refuse to pay my bills?

In my work am I just, hard-working, honest? Do I cheat or break agreements?

Do I drive dangerously? Have I driven when under the influence of drink?

Have I been truthful and fair? Have I deliberately deceived others? Judged them rashly? Injured their reputation by lies about them? Have I revealed secrets?

Have I been guilty of physical violence? Have I been cruel?
Do I forgive people - or keep up long-standing
resentments? Do I insult others, quarrel with them, lose
my temper?

Have I been responsible for advising an abortion or
procuring one?

Have I stolen the property of others or planned to get hold
of what belongs to another?

**'If any man would come after me, let him deny
himself and take up his cross and follow me.'**

Do I accept responsibility for my own life and destiny?

Do I eat or drink more than is reasonable?

Am I envious, proud and arrogant?

Do I complain about misfortunes? Have I freely accepted
from God the many people, events and injustices of today
and of my past life, with an open, and willing spirit.

Have I been chaste and pure? Or have I toyed with
temptations to impurity - by deliberately looking for what
is impure?

Have I given in to sensuality, particularly in my reading
or my entertainments?

Is my married life according to God's will and law? Have
I used methods of birth control contrary to the Church's
teaching on the place of sex in marriage?

Have I failed to follow my conscience out of fear or
hypocrisy?

Desire for conversion

The two most important things you do in the celebration of the Sacrament of Penance are to be sorry for what you have done wrong and to make up your mind not to do it again. This is not necessarily a matter of feeling tearful about your sins, nor yet again does it mean that you have to try to shut out of your mind the possibility that you will in fact fall again. It is much more a matter of really and genuinely making up your mind to try to live your whole life in the light of the Gospel and of the holiness and love of God.

The Ten Commandments of God

1. I am the Lord your God: you shall not have strange gods before me.

2. You shall not take the name of the Lord your God in vain.

3. Remember to keep holy the Lord's day.

4. Honour your father and your mother.

5. You shall not kill.

6. You shall not commit adultery.

7. You shall not steal.

8. You shall not bear false witness against your neighbour.

9. You shall not covet your neighbour's wife.

10. You shall not covet your neighbour's goods.

The Six Chief Commandments of the Church

1. To keep the Sundays and holy days of Obligation holy, by hearing Mass and resting from servile works.

2. To keep the days of Fasting and Abstinence appointed by the Church.

3. To go to Confession when we are conscious of having sinned gravely.

4. To receive the Blessed Sacrament at least once a year, at Easter or thereabouts.

5. To contribute to the support of our pastors.

6. Not to marry within certain degrees of kindred without dispensation.

Going to Confession

The Penitent is received

You will now be ready to approach the Priest. He welcomes you warmly in brotherly love. You make the sign of the cross, saying:

In the name of the Father, and of the Son, and of the Holy Spirit. Amen.

The Priest will then briefly invite you to have confidence and trust in God.

This is the point in confession for you to tell the Priest about yourself, if you are someone he does not already know. You should tell him anything which may help him to help you in your spiritual life; for instance, when you last went to confession, whether you are married or not, and the main difficulties which you have in trying to live the Christian life.

The Word of God

Next the Priest, or you yourself at his invitation, may choose to read an appropriate passage of Holy Scripture proclaiming God's mercy and calling men to conversion. (Some suitable ones appear at pp. 33-38). This reading is not necessary if you have read the Word of God in your private preparation.

Confession, counsel and reconciliation

Where it is the custom, you now say a general formula for confession (for example: The Confiteor, see p. 39). You then confess your sins. You may speak in a normal conversational manner. Listen to any advice the Priest may give you, and ask him questions if you do not understand anything.

The Priest proposes a penance which you accept to make satisfaction for sin and to amend your life. This penance will serve not only to make up for the past but also to help you begin a new life and provide you with the antidote to weakness. As far as possible, the penance will correspond to the seriousness and nature of the sins. It may suitably take the form of prayer, self-denial, and especially service of your neighbour and works of mercy. These will underline the fact that sin and its forgiveness have a social aspect.

Your prayer of sorrow

The Priest will then ask you to express your sorrow. You may use one of the following prayers of sorrow or any other act of contrition you prefer (see pp. 39-40):

O my God, because you are so good, I am very sorry that I have sinned against you, and with the help of your grace I will not sin again.

O my God, I am sorry and beg pardon for all my sins, and detest them above all things, because they deserve your dreadful punishments, because they have crucified my loving Saviour Jesus Christ, and, most of all, because they offend your infinite goodness; and I firmly resolve, by the help of your grace, never to offend you again, and carefully to avoid the occasions of sin.

O my God, I am heartily sorry for all my sins, because they offend you, who are infinitely good, and I firmly resolve, with the help of your grace, never to offend you again.

Absolution

If you are not kneeling, bow your head as the Priest extends his hands and pronounces the words of absolution, as follows:

God, the Father of mercies, through the death and resurrection of his Son has reconciled the world to himself and sent the Holy Spirit among us for the forgiveness of sins; through the ministry of the Church may God give you pardon and peace, and I absolve you from your sins in the name of the Father, and of the Son, and of the Holy Spirit. Amen.

Conclusion of the Rite

After absolution, the Priest may continue:
Give thanks to the Lord, for he is good.
You reply: His mercy endures forever.

Then the Priest dismisses you saying:
The Lord has freed you from your sins. Go in peace.

You reply: Thanks be to God.

Thanksgiving

At the conclusion of the rite you leave the place of confession. No matter what the penance given you was, you now have the opportunity to reflect on what has taken place and to thank God for his mercy and forgiveness in the quiet of the church or wherever you may be.

You are once again part of the mystery of salvation.

Here is a prayer of thanksgiving (see also pp. 41-43):

Almighty and merciful God, how wonderfully you created man and still more wonderfully remade him. You do not abandon the sinner but seek him out with a father's love. You sent your Son into the world to destroy sin and death by his passion, and to restore life and joy by his resurrection. You sent the Holy Spirit into my heart making me one of your children and an heir of your kingdom. You constantly renew my spirit in the sacraments of your redeeming love, freeing me from slavery to sin and transforming me ever more closely into the likeness of your beloved Son. Thank you for the wonder of your mercy. Glory to you through Christ, in the Holy Spirit, now and forever. Amen.

SCRIPTURE PASSAGES

De Profundis

Out of the depths I cry to you, O Lord,
Lord, hear my voice!
O let your ears be attentive
to the voice of my pleading.
If you, O Lord, should mark our guilt,
Lord, who would survive?
But with you is found forgiveness;
for this we revere you.
My soul is waiting for the Lord,
I count on his word.
My soul is longing for the Lord,
more than watchmen for daybreak.
Let the watchman count on daybreak
and Israel on the Lord.
Because with the Lord there is mercy
and fullness of redemption,
Israel indeed he will redeem from all its iniquity.
(*Psalm* 130)

Be perfect like your heavenly Father

'For I tell you, if your virtue goes no deeper than that of the scribes and Pharisees, you will never get into the kingdom of heaven.

'You have learnt how it was said to our ancestors: You must not kill; and if anyone does kill he must answer for it before the court. But I say this to you: anyone who is angry with his brother will answer for it before the court; if a man calls his brother "Fool" he will answer for it before the Sanhedrin; and if a man calls him "Renegade" he will answer for it in hell fire. So then, if you are bringing your offering to the altar and there remember that your brother has something against you, leave your offering there before the altar, go and be reconciled with your brother first, and then come back and present your offering. Come to terms with your opponent in good time while you are still on the way to the court with him, or he may hand you over to the judge and the judge to the officer, and you will be thrown into prison. I tell you solemnly, you will not get out till you have paid the last penny.

'You have learnt how it was said: You must not commit adultery. But I say this to you: if a man looks at a woman lustfully, he has already committed adultery with her in his heart. If your right eye should cause you to sin, tear it out and throw it away; for it will do you less harm to lose one part of you than to have your whole body thrown into hell. And if your right hand should cause you to sin, cut it off and throw it away; for it will do you less harm to lose one part of you than to have your whole body go to hell.

'It has also been said: Anyone who divorces his wife must give her a writ of dismissal. But I say this to you: everyone who divorces his wife, except for the case of fornication, makes her an adulteress; and anyone who marries a divorced woman commits adultery.

'Again, you have learnt how it was said to our ancestors: You must not break your oath, but must fulfil your oaths to the Lord. But I say this to you: do not swear at all, either by heaven, since that is God's throne; or by the earth, since that is his footstool; or by Jerusalem, since that is the city of the great king. Do not swear by your own head either, since you cannot turn a single hair white or black. All you need say is "Yes" if you mean yes, "No" if you mean no; anything more than this comes from the evil one.

'You have learnt how it was said: Eye for eye and tooth for tooth. But I say this to you: offer the wicked man no resistance. On the contrary, if anyone hits you on the right cheek, offer him the other as well; if a man takes you to law and would have your tunic, let him have your cloak as well. And if anyone orders you to go one mile, go two miles with him. Give to anyone who asks, and if anyone wants to borrow, do not turn away.

'You have learnt how it was said: You must love your neighbour and hate your enemy. But I say this to you: love your enemies and pray for those who persecute you; in this way you will be sons of your Father in heaven, for he causes his sun to rise on bad men as well as good, and his rain to fall on honest and dishonest men alike. For if you love those who love you, what right have you to claim any credit? Even the tax collectors do as much, do they not? And if you save your greetings for your brothers, are you doing anything exceptional? Even the pagans do as much, do they not? You must therefore be perfect just as your heavenly Father is perfect'. (*Mt* 5:20-48)

Never repay evil with evil

Bless those who persecute you: never curse them, bless them. Rejoice with those who rejoice and be sad with those in sorrow. Treat everyone with equal kindness; never be condescending but make real friends with the poor. Do not allow yourself to become self-satisfied. Never repay evil with evil but let everyone see that you are interested only in the highest ideals. Do all you can to live at peace with everyone. Never try to get revenge; leave that, my friends, to God's anger. As scripture says: vengeance is mine - I will pay them back, the Lord promises. But there is more: If your enemy is hungry, you should give him food, and if he is thirsty, let him drink. Thus you heap red-hot coals on his head. Resist evil and conquer it with good. (*Rom* 12:14-21)

Give up your old way of life

In particular, I want to urge you in the name of the Lord, not to go on living the aimless kind of life that pagans live. Intellectually they are in the dark, and they are estranged from the life of God, without knowledge because they have shut their hearts to it. Their sense of right and wrong once dulled, they have abandoned themselves to sexuality and eagerly pursue a career of indecency of every kind. Now that is hardly the way you have learnt from Christ, unless you failed to hear him properly when you were taught what the truth is in Jesus. You must give up your old way of life; you must put aside your old self, which gets corrupted by following illusory desires. Your mind must be renewed by a spiritual revolution so that you can put on the new self that has been created in God's way, in the goodness and holiness of the truth.

So from now on, there must be no more lies: You must speak the truth to one another, since we are all parts of one another. Even if you are angry, you must not sin: never let the sun set on your anger or else you will give the devil a foothold. Anyone who was a thief must stop stealing; he should try to find some useful manual work instead, and be able to do some good by helping others that are in need. Guard against foul talk; let your words be for the improvement of others, as occasion offers, and do good to your listeners, otherwise you will only be grieving the

Holy Spirit of God who has marked you with his seal for you to be set free when the day comes. Never have grudges against others, or lose your temper, or raise your voice to anybody, or call each other names, or allow any sort of spitefulness. Be friends with one another, and kind, forgiving each other as readily as God forgave you in Christ. (*Eph* 4:17-32)

PRAYERS OF PENANCE AND THANKSGIVING

The Confiteor

I confess to almighty God, that I have sinned through my own fault, in my thoughts and in my words, in what I have done, and in what I have failed to do; and I ask blessed Mary, ever virgin, and all the angels and saints, to pray for me to the Lord our God.

Prayers of sorrow

Father of mercy, like the prodigal son I return to you and say: 'I have sinned against you and am no longer worthy to be called your son'. Christ Jesus, Saviour of the world, I pray with the repentant thief to whom you promised Paradise: 'Lord, remember me in your kingdom'. Holy Spirit, fountain of love, I call on you with trust: 'Purify my heart, and help me to walk as a child of light'.

Lord Jesus, you chose to be called the friend of sinners. By your saving death and resurrection free me from my sins. May your peace take root in my heart and bring forth a harvest of love, holiness, and truth.

Lord Jesus Christ, you are the Lamb of God; you take away the sins of the world. Through the grace of the Holy Spirit restore me to friendship with your Father, cleanse me from every stain of sin in the blood you shed for me, for the glory of your name.

My God, I am sorry for my sins with all my heart, in choosing to do wrong and failing to do good, I have sinned against you whom I should love above all things. I firmly intend, with your help, to do penance, to sin no more, and to avoid whatever leads me to sin. Our Saviour, Jesus Christ, suffered and died for us; in his name, my God, have mercy.

O God, loose, remit, and forgive my sins against you, whether in word, in deed, or in thought;
and whether they are willingly or unwillingly,
knowingly or unknowingly committed, forgive them all.
For you are good and you love all human beings.
And through the prayers of your most holy Mother,
or your heavenly servants and holy spirits,
and all the Saints who have found favour with you,
enable me to receive without condemnation your holy Body and your Precious Blood.
Let my soul and body be thus healed and my evil imaginings be driven away,
for yours is the kingdom,
the power, and the glory:

Father, Son, and Holy Spirit,
now and forever. Amen

The Memorare

Remember, O most loving Virgin Mary, that it is a thing unheard of, that anyone ever had recourse to your protection, implored your help, or sought your intercession, and was left forsaken. Filled therefore with confidence in your goodness I fly to you, O Mother, Virgin of virgins. To you I come, before you I stand, a sorrowful sinner. Despise not my poor words, O Mother of the Word of God, but graciously hear and grant my prayer. Amen.

Prayers of thanksgiving

God and Father of us all, you have forgiven my sins and sent me your peace. Help me to forgive my neighbour and to work with the people I meet to establish peace and unity in this world. Amen.

Lord God, creator and ruler of your kingdom of light, in your great love for this world you gave up your only Son for our salvation. His cross has redeemed mankind, his death has given us life, his resurrection has raised us to glory. Teach me to be reverent in the presence of your glory; fill my heart with faith, my days with good works, my life with your love; may your truth be on my lips and your wisdom in all my actions, that I may receive the reward of everlasting life. Amen.

Prayer before a Crucifix

Behold, O kind and most sweet Jesus, I cast myself on my knees in your sight, and with the most fervent desire of my soul, I pray and beseech you that you would impress upon my heart lively sentiments of faith, hope, and charity, with a true repentance for my sins, and a firm desire of amendment, while with deep affection and grief of soul I ponder within myself and mentally contemplate your five most precious wounds; having before my eyes that which David spoke in prophecy of you, O good Jesus: 'They pierced my hands and my feet; they have numbered all my bones'.

Prayer of Firm Purpose of Amendment

O Lord, I place myself in your hands and dedicate myself to you. I pledge myself to do your will in all things: To love the Lord God with all my heart, all my soul, all my strength. Not to kill. Not to steal. Not to covet. Not to bear false witness. To honour all persons. Not to do to another what I would not wish done to myself. To chastise the body. Not to seek after pleasures. To love fasting. To relieve the poor. To clothe the naked. To visit the sick. To bury the dead. To help in trouble. To console the sorrowing. To hold myself aloof from worldly ways. To prefer nothing to the love of Christ. Not to give way to anger. Not to foster a desire for revenge. Not to entertain deceit in the heart. Not to make a false peace. Not to forsake charity. Not to swear, lest I swear falsely. To speak the truth with heart and tongue. Not to return evil for evil. To do no injury: yes, even to bear patiently any injury done to me. To love my enemies. Not to curse those who curse me, but rather to bless them. To bear persecution for justice' sake. Not to be proud. Not to be given to intoxicating drink. Not to be an over-eater. Not to be lazy. Not to be slothful. Not to be a murmurer. Not to be a detractor. To put my trust in God. To refer the good I see in myself to God. To refer any evil in myself to myself. To fear the day of judgment. To be in dread of hell. To desire eternal life with spiritual longing. To keep death before my eyes daily. To keep constant watch over my actions. To remember that God sees me everywhere. To call upon Christ for defense against evil thoughts that arise in my heart. To guard my tongue against wicked speech. To avoid much speaking. To avoid idle talk. To read only what is good to read. To look at only what is good to see. To pray often. To ask forgiveness daily for my sins, and to seek ways to amend my life. To obey my superiors in all things rightful. Not to desire to be thought holy, but to seek holiness. To fulfill the commandments of God by good works. To love chastity. To hate no one. Not to be jealous or envious of anyone. Not to love strife. Not to love pride. To honour the aged. To pray for my enemies. To make peace after a quarrel, before the setting of the sun. Never to despair of your mercy, O God of Mercy. Amen.

Prayer of Abandonment

Father, I abandon myself into your hands;
Do with me what you will.
Whatever you may do, I thank you;
I am ready for all, I accept all.
Let only your will be done in me and in all your creatures.
I wish no more than this, O Lord.
Into your hands I commend my soul:
I offer it to you with all the love of my heart,
for I love you, Lord, and so need to give myself,
to surrender myself into your hands without reserve
and with boundless confidence, for you are my Father.

Act of Faith, Hope and Love

My God, I believe in you,
I trust in you,
I love you above all things,
with all my heart and mind and strength.
I love you because you are supremely
good and worth loving;
and because I love you,
I am sorry with all my heart for offending you.
Lord, have mercy on me, a sinner.
Amen.

Prayer to St Michael

St Michael, the Archangel, defend us in the day of battle; be our safeguard against the wickedness and snares of the devil. May God rebuke him, we humbly pray and do you, O Prince of the heavenly host, by the power of God, cast into hell Satan and all the other evil spirits who prowl through the world seeking the ruin of souls. Amen.

REDISCOVERING PENANCE
AND RECONCILIATION

This sacrament has many names, and is commonly known as Confession. While Confession itself forms an essential part of the sacrament, it is not all of it. It is more accurately known as the Sacrament of conversion in which we respond to Christ's call to return to the Father; of forgiveness since the Priest grants us Christ's pardon and peace; of reconciliation, where we are reconciled to God and our neighbour.

Call to continuous conversion

If Baptism forgives my sins, then as a baptised person why should I need this Sacrament? St John wrote, 'If we say we have no sin, we deceive ourselves and the truth is not in us'. Baptism does not abolish human frailty and weakness, nor our inclination to sin. The struggle of the Christian therefore is one of daily conversion, to become with Christ's help, more and more like him. Our first conversion takes place at our Baptism, it is true - there we renounced evil, received new life and forgiveness of our sins. But throughout all of our life, thereafter, Christ's call to continuous conversion echoes on. There is an uninterrupted process which goes on - a second conversion - in which we are helped to walk the path of penance and renewal every day with the help of our mother, the Church.

Conversion is not just a human work. It is a gift of God given to the contrite heart - by God who loved us first. It does not mean changing faith. It involves an acknowledgement of our condition and a willingness to change the direction in which we are going. It is not a quick or superficial process, but deep and can take as long as is required.

Radical reorientation

At the centre of this Sacrament is conversion of the heart, interior conversion. That is its aim and its gift, what it contributes to our Christian journey on this earth. The new Catechism describes interior repentance as a radical reorientation of our whole life, a return, a conversion to God with all our heart, an end to sin, a turning away from evil, with repugnance towards the evil actions we have committed. At the same time it entails the desire and resolution to change one's life, with hope in God's mercy and trust in the help of his grace.

The human heart, it continues, is heavy and hardened. God must give man a new heart. Conversion is first of all a work of God's grace who makes our hearts return to him.

To touch on this Sacrament is to talk in these terms, in this language which is profound and requires sincerity, thoughtfulness and careful reflection on our part.

Where do repentance, conversion, sin and God's grace fit into our vocabulary and daily life? The Church and Christian experience testify that they are central elements of our existence, and this Sacrament - often called the refreshing waters of a second Baptism - plays an important role in the Christian's pilgrim journey.

Forgiveness and reconciliation

How does the Sacrament of Penance help us to participate in this process of conversion? By enabling us to receive the forgiveness of God and to be reconciled with the Church, the community.

Though, perhaps, not immediately obvious, these two elements are most important and inseparable; they answer directly the trouble we face since sin is before all else an offence against God and ruptures communion with him, and at the same time damages communion with his body the Church, the Christian community, your neighbour.

It is very true that only God forgives sins; Christ as Son of Man forgave sins by exercising his divine power, and he in turn gave this power to man to exercise in his name. Christ willed his Church to be the sign and instrument of the forgiveness and reconciliation he won for us. He entrusted the power of absolution to the apostolic ministry - to Bishops and Priests - on his behalf - and also the authority to reconcile sinners with his Church.

Conversion, prayer and penance

Over the centuries, this Sacrament has undergone changes in how it was celebrated. Fundamentally, however, it has never changed in two aspects: first, the sinner is helped towards conversion with the action of the Holy Spirit through contrition, confession and what is called satisfaction or penance. Second, God acts in the sinner's favour through the intervention of his Church who forgives, prays and does penance with the sinner.

Contrition

Contrition means sorrow and detestation for the sins you have committed and a resolve, leaning on God's help, not to sin again. It presupposes a willingness to prepare for the Sacrament by examining your conscience. This is important, and can at times be difficult for people. It is often best done in the light of the Word of God - by taking or listening to a passage from the Gospel or New Testament letters, or especially the Sermon on the Mount.

Confession

Confession is to disclose your sins to a Priest. On a human level this frees us and facilitates reconciliation with others, but by admitting and looking squarely at our own sins we take responsibility for them opening ourselves again to God, our neighbour and a new beginning. In confessing to God's appointed minister, we can act in the sure faith that we confess to Christ himself through his Church. Here we can take great courage. We can confess sincerely, with humility - for if the sick person is too ashamed to show his wounds to the doctor, the medicine cannot heal what it does not know.

Mercy produces mercy

Regular confession is recommended. Confession to the same confessor also. Why? Because it helps us form our conscience, fight against selfish and evil tendencies, and opens us to Christ's healing and to progress in the life of the Spirit - to become more and more like our Master. The constant receiving of mercy helps us in turn to be merciful as he is merciful.

Repairing harm done

The Sacrament certainly calls on and helps us to do all we can to repair the harm our sins have done to our neighbour. For example, by returning things we have stolen, asking forgiveness of someone we have hurt. Because the sinner himself is also weakened, his life disordered and injured by sin, the Sacrament further helps him to recover by making amends, to expiate his sins. This satisfaction is also known as a penance, given by the confessor Priest, and is often either prayer, an offering, works of mercy, service to your neighbour, voluntary self-denial, sacrifices, and especially patient acceptance of our own particular cross. This call helps us to become more and more like Christ.

Fruits and benefits

To conclude, the benefits of this Sacrament are enormous. It restores us, in a way we can live and experience stage by stage, to God's grace and joins us to him in close friendship - we are reconciled to God. A sincere and modest approach to this Sacrament is usually followed by peace, consolation and a serene conscience - a small resurrection from death. In a way which we may not readily recognise, the sacrament revitalises the life of the Church as as a whole; it restores and repairs fraternal communion damaged by our sins.

Pope John Paul II says that the forgiven penitent is reconciled with himself in his innermost being, where he regains his innermost truth. He is reconciled with his brethren whom he has in some way offended and wounded. He is reconciled with the Church and he is reconciled with all creation.

Preparing for the Sacrament

To help bring about this real change of heart, the Church has now made it possible for there to be much less formality about receiving the Sacrament of Penance than in the past; she encourages the Priest to welcome each penitent in a friendly and personal way; she permits the use of an ordinary room in the church rather than a confessional box, and she gives us the opportunity of seeing the Priest face to face if we want to.

With the same objective of helping us to 'conversion of heart', the Priest is now encouraged to read to the penitent a short passage from Holy Scripture. This will be chosen to help us recognise our sinfulness as we are called once again to try to live our lives according to the holiness and love of God.

Ways to help

The Church recognises the dangers in mere routine repetition of the Sacrament, and so she provides a rich variety of choice to suit our spiritual needs at different times; even if we always go to the same Priest (generally a good thing to do) details of the celebration of the Sacrament will change as he sees growth and change taking place in our determination to be ever renewed in the way of Our Lord.

As in the past, the ordinary and usual way to receive the Sacrament is by going individually to confession. The revised rite provides also for communal celebrations leading to individual confession and absolution. In unusual circumstances there may be a similar service with general absolution. There is no doubt that attending communal celebrations will aid our understanding of the need for a continual conversion to God. We ought to make every effort to attend when such services are arranged.